Science Based On Philosophy

Relationship between Science and Philosophy

Jack Bracknell

Contents

INTRODUCTION

Quite literally, the term "philosophy" means, "love of wisdom." In a broad sense, philosophy is an activity people undertake when they seek to understand fundamental truths about themselves, the world in which they live, and their relationships to the world and to each other.

Philosophy explains, examines and interprets the full meaning of scientific achievements with a view to solving the riddle of the universe as a whole for finding out the key to the 'mystery' to the universe. Science is concerned with facts as they appear to us

Philosophy may be called the "science of sciences" probably in the sense that it is, in effect, the self-awareness of the sciences and the source from which all the sciences draw their world-view and methodological principles, which in the course of centuries have been honed down into concise forms.

PASSION FOR WISDOM

The name "philosophy" comes from the Greek words "phileo" - love and "sophia" - wisdom, which means love of wisdom, wisdom. This literal meaning seems to be far from the real meaning of the concept "philosophy". However, this is only partly true. Wisdom still remains an essential definition of philosophical thinking. Philosophy is wisdom, but not of an individual, but of the united Mind of people. In other words, philosophy is collective thinking. What does it mean?

First, philosophy is precisely thinking, and not cognition, not feeling, not believing, not willing, not acting.

Secondly, philosophy is not just thinking, but co-thinking, i.e. such thinking, which presupposes the thinking communication of people or the thinking of people together. Philosophy is collective thinking just as science is collective knowledge, art is collective feeling, religion is collective belief, morality-politics-law is collective will, economics is collective production-distribution, etc.

Thirdly, the starting and ending point of philosophizing is not knowledge, not goodness, not beauty, but a thought that has meaning for many other people, primarily for the philosophers themselves. Of course, people think collectively in science, in art, and in all other spheres of human activity. But this collective thinking is only a subordinate element of the scientific-cognitive, artistic, etc. activities. It is philosophical only to the extent that it is internally free, not directly connected with the production of knowledge, beauty, material wealth, etc.

 In philosophy, collective thinking is self-sufficient, as far as possible removed from the solution of cognitive-artistic-practical problems. The element of philosophy is the element of pure, self-sufficient thought [(1) - hereinafter, the number in brackets indicates a note placed at the end of the book]. If philosophers offer something to non-philosophers, then it is by no means ready-made answers-recipes, but their semi-finished products. After all, a thought-idea is always a semi-finished product...

Previously, some philosophers, writers and scientists put forward a position about philosophy as a science of sciences. This position, while correctly emphasizing the special role of philosophy in comparison with the particular sciences as a general worldview, methodological, ideological basis of scientific knowledge, at the same time suffers from a significant flaw. It declares philosophy a science and thereby establishes a rigid connection between philosophical ideas and scientific theories. In fact, philosophy is a special form of thinking. It includes an element of science, but is not limited to a scientific form of knowledge. Science is a form of collective knowledge, while philosophy is a form of collective thinking of people.

what is connected in the object (2). On the contrary, the controlling and transforming activity carries out the "translation" of the ideal into the material plane [objectification]. In this activity, the subject seeks to separate what is connected and connect what is divided. Thought, on the ideal, mental level, carries out the interaction [mutual transition, mutual mediation] of these oppositely directed forms of activity. It is therefore not reducible to any of these forms of activity.) mutual mediation] of these oppositely directed forms of activity. It is therefore not reducible to any of these forms of activity.) mutual mediation] of these oppositely directed forms of activity. It is therefore not reducible to any of these forms of activity.)

In addition, philosophy, unlike science, cannot oblige, prescribe, indicate "how it should be", be a legislator. Its provisions have only advisory power in relation to other branches of human activity. The expression "philosophy is the science of sciences" reflects just an attempt to present philosophy as the legislator of the sciences, dictating its will to them, how to behave This expression is also incorrect in the sense that it limits the relationship of philosophy with other branches of human activity only to the area of relations with the sciences (3). Philosophy as a form of collective thinking is directly related to science, and to art, and to material practice, and to the management of society, and to the individual experience of a person. It reflects on all these forms of activity, occupying the position of the center or focus in which all forms of human activity converge. In other words, philosophy is the focus, the center of all human strivings and darings.

In our country, philosophy has long been (and still is) strongly tied to the state and science. Philosophical research is carried out to a large extent within or under the auspices of the Russian Academy of Sciences. The non-differentiation of philosophy from science leads it to unjustified learning, a kind of philosophical scientism. Scientific language in philosophical books and articles is a very common phenomenon. As a result, the same is expected from philosophical research-reflections as from scientific research. The flip side of this approach, i.e. The desire to "teach" philosophy is the expectation from it of some specific scientific results, ready-made answers to the questions posed by life. Since this expectation is not justified, philosophy is disappointed.

Science, as we have already said, is concerned with knowledge; philosophy knows nothing. It only comprehends the course and results of knowledge (and not only knowledge, but also practice, art, in general, all human experience). Science is scientific, and philosophy is philosophical! Science produces knowledge. Philosophy, on the other hand, produces and develops ideas (4). No more. Philosophical ideas are ideas of ideas: scientific, artistic, practical, etc. Accordingly, philosophizing does not directly serve knowledge, practice, art, but rather indirectly.

Philosophy in our country must find its own face and finally free itself from external fetters. No one, neither scientific authorities, nor statesmen, nor religious figures, should interfere in the affairs of philosophy.

An example of scientification, scientification of philosophy are the attempts of some philosophers and philosophical schools to express the basic philosophical provisions in the form of laws. Since laws are discovered in science, it means that it can be done in philosophy as well. The most striking example of the invention of philosophical laws are the Marxist laws of dialectics. From our point of view, only science can claim to discover and study the laws of the subject area. In philosophy, "law" is only one of the categories, paired with the category "phenomenon", and to call some philosophical principles with the same term is a logical mistake. Either we must admit that "law" is the highest category of dialectics, or we must admit that the word "law" in the case when we are talking about the "law of dialectics" has a different meaning than when it denotes one of the categories of dialectics.

One of the reasons for using the concept of "law" in Marxist philosophy in relation to some of its main provisions is precisely the voluntary or involuntary drawing of an analogy between philosophy and science.

I would also like to draw attention to this side of the question of the laws of dialectics. Our world is a probabilistic world, and chance plays no less a role in it than necessity, regularity. The expression "laws of dialectics", whether we like it or not, focuses on the knowledge of regularity, orderliness of the real world and leaves in the shade another, directly opposite side of it: disorder, variety of phenomena, stochastics. And this creates a well-known bias towards mechanistic, Laplacian determinism, which absolutizes necessity, regularity, orderliness. A bias in philosophical thinking leads to a bias in any other thinking: political, economic, managerial... Doesn't this explain that for decades in our country the cult of the plan, the cult of the clerks, has been created? administrative methods of management and underestimated the importance of stochastic mechanisms, in particular, the market, the election system? We mainly talked about consciousness, organization, planning, and fought against spontaneity.

But spontaneity is to a certain extent just as important as planning and organization. Human society is a living system, and it does not need a rigid order that implies a system of rigid determination of people's behavior, but a living order-disorder that takes into account equally necessity and chance, unity and diversity, general and particular as well as planning and organization. Human society is a living system, and it does not need a rigid order that implies a system of rigid determination of people's behavior, but a living order-disorder that takes into account equally necessity and chance, unity and diversity, general and particular. as well as planning and organization.

Human society is a living system, and it does not need a rigid order that implies a system of rigid determination of people's behavior, but a living order-disorder that takes into account equally necessity and chance, unity and diversity, general and particular.

The lifelessness of the concept of the laws of dialectics is especially evident in the example of the law of negation of negation. The concept of this law imposes on us a rigidly unambiguous (almost in the spirit of Laplacian determinism) scheme of the direction of development, formation. It, in essence, excludes the element of chance in the emergence of the new, the multivariance of the ways of development, formation. The concept of the law of negation of negation is vulnerable in another respect. This law is usually defined as a law that characterizes the direction of the development process, the unity of the emergence of the new and the relative repetition of some moments of the old (see: Philosophical Encyclopedic Dictionary. M., 1983. P. 471).

Meanwhile, if you think about it, the law of negation of negation cannot fully characterize the direction of development. Indeed, in any development (becoming), the most important moment is the transition from the old to the new, i.e. constructive movement from one positive content to another. In the law of the negation of negation, the emphasis is on negation, even if it is a second negation that denies the first. Yes, indeed, the new denies the old. But this is only a moment of the relation of the new to the old. The new has another positive content, which is not (never was!) in the old, and this content is by no means fully revealed by the concept of negation.

The affirmation of the new does not follow from the denial of the old, otherwise the anarchists and all sorts of nihilist deniers would be right. Negation always remains a negation, no matter how it is called: subtraction, dialectical negation, second negation. (In Hegelian philosophy, negation had the meaning of a positive concept, since this philosophy is characterized by a circularity of ideas - the absolute, world spirit eventually returns to itself). In the concept of negation, if we evaluate it realistically, the negative content always comes to the fore.

Otherwise, this concept would be denoted by a different word.

 Of course, there is a difference between negation as destruction-annihilation and negation as a moment of development. But this does not give us the right to consider dialectical negation as such a moment that makes development development, and becoming - becoming. The "law" of negation of negation reflects only the fact of negation and continuity between the new and the old. The relationship between the old and the new is fully characterized by the categories of development and formation. No artificial props, at least in the form of the "law of negation of negation", is not required to explain the meaning of these categories. If we talk about the disclosure of the content of the categories "development" and "becoming", then it should be said that this content is revealed in a whole system of categories and concepts.

Speaking about the fact that philosophy does not know anything, we had in mind that the "ecological niche" of philosophy as a special type of culture is not knowledge, but thinking. The goal of philosophizing is not the comprehension of truth, but wisdom. After all, philosophizing is philosophizing (in the good sense of the word). Only science "has the right" to engage in cognition. This is her feature, her "bread". They may say: what about the expressions "philosophical knowledge", "philosophical science", etc.? To this we will answer: the words "knowledge" and "science" in relation to philosophy are used in a different sense than when they speak of science as a type of culture and of knowledge as a branch of human activity. Indeed, even in theology, the expressions "theological knowledge", "theological science" are often used. But no one considers "theological knowledge" to be scientific knowledge, When people talk about philosophical knowledge, they do not mean the knowledge that is acquired in the process of scientific knowledge.

Philosophical knowledge and scientific knowledge are different "things". Scientific knowledge is the result of cognition of the real world, the world as an object of cognition. Philosophical knowledge is the result of intra-philosophical information flows from one philosopher to another. If I read the writings of Plato and understood them, then I gained knowledge about the teachings of Plato, about his ideas, views, and so on. The sum of philosophical knowledge is, first of all, knowledge of the basic philosophical teachings-ideas of the past and present.

Philosophical knowledge is similar to scientific knowledge in the sense that, like scientific knowledge, it more or less adequately reflects the subject, in our case, the teaching, ideas, thoughts of another philosopher (other philosophers). A philosophically educated person is a person who more or less adequately perceived and assimilated the main ideas of the philosophers of the past and present. Philosophical education is the basis of philosophical learning and philosophical professionalism.

The words "scholarship" and "scientist" in relation to the philosopher mean only that the person thoroughly studied philosophy. Almost the same can be said about the words "scientific" and "science". When applied to philosophy, these words mean the learning of philosophy. In addition, the word "science" in combination with the adjective "philosophical" (philosophical science) means one or another branch of philosophy that has become a relatively independent philosophical discipline, a branch of philosophical knowledge. Philosophical sciences are called ethics, aesthetics, logic... Philosophical education is the basis of philosophical learning and philosophical professionalism. The words "scholarship" and "scientist" in relation to the philosopher mean only that the person thoroughly studied philosophy. Almost the same can be said about the words "scientific" and "science".

When applied to philosophy, these words mean the learning of philosophy. In addition, the word "science" in combination with the adjective "philosophical" (philosophical science) means one or another branch of philosophy that has become a relatively independent philosophical discipline, a branch of philosophical knowledge. Philosophical sciences are called ethics, aesthetics, logic... Philosophical education is the basis of philosophical learning and philosophical professionalism. The words "scholarship" and "scientist" in relation to the philosopher mean only that the person thoroughly studied philosophy. Almost the same can be said about the words "scientific" and "science". When applied to philosophy, these words mean the learning of philosophy. In addition, the word "science" in combination with the adjective "philosophical" (philosophical science) means one or another branch of philosophy that has become a relatively independent philosophical discipline, a branch of philosophical knowledge. Philosophical sciences are called ethics, aesthetics, logic... When applied to philosophy, these words mean the learning of philosophy.

In addition, the word "science" in combination with the adjective "philosophical" (philosophical science) means one or another branch of philosophy that has become a relatively independent philosophical discipline, a branch of philosophical knowledge. Philosophical sciences are called ethics, aesthetics, logic... When applied to philosophy, these words mean the learning of philosophy. In addition, the word "science" in combination with the adjective "philosophical" (philosophical science) means one or another branch of philosophy that has become a relatively independent philosophical discipline, a branch of philosophical knowledge. Philosophical sciences are called ethics, aesthetics, logic...

In recent years, another extreme has made itself felt: anti-scientism-irrationalism. It is definitely a reaction to previous decades of philosophical scientism-rationalism. The liberated philosophers suddenly started talking like theologians, mystics, clairvoyants, prophets...

Neither scientism nor anti-scientism makes a philosopher a philosopher. We, philosophers, must learn to speak with our own voice, without scientism and scientism, on the one hand, and without religious-mystical, prophetic rhetoric-affection, on the other.

2. SUBJECT AND "PARTS" OF PHILOSOPHY

Philosophers have been discussing the problem of the "parts" of philosophy, its structuring since the initial accumulation of philosophical ideas took place and the first systematic philosophers appeared.

Here are some quotes from ancient authors:

Seneca(mid-1st century AD): "Most of those who wrote about it, and the greatest ones, argued that philosophy is divided into three parts: moral, natural, and that dedicated to the human mind (5). The first brings order to the soul. The second examines the nature of things. The third tests the properties of words, their arrangement, types of evidence, so that a lie does not creep in under the guise of truth" (6).

Diogenes Laertes(early III century AD): "Finally, some philosophers are called physicists, for the study of nature; others - ethics, for reasoning about mores; still others - dialecticians, for the intricacies of speeches. Physics, ethics and dialectics are the three parts of philosophy; physics teaches about the world and everything that it contains; ethics - about the life and properties of a person; dialectics, on the other hand, takes care of the arguments for both physics and ethics. Before Archelaus [inclusive] there was only one genus - physics; from Socrates ... ethics originates; from Zeno of Elea - dialectics" (7).

Sextus Empiricus(late II-early III century AD): "since philosophy is some motley thing, for the purposes of a harmonious and methodical study of each point, it will be necessary to consider at least a little about the parts of philosophy.

To get straight to the point, some, as you know, accept it as consisting of one part, others - from two, and still others - from three. Of those who accept one part, some admit the physical part, others the ethical part, still others the logical part. And likewise, of those who divide it in two, some have divided it into physical and logical parts, others into physical and ethical parts, and still others into logical and ethical parts. And those who divided it into three parts accordingly divided it into physical, logical and ethical" (p. 61).

"Perfect in comparison with them are those who said that one thing in philosophy is something physical, another is ethical, and a third is logical. The initiator of this, in principle, is Plato ... The students of Xenocrates, the Peripatetics, and also the Stoics adhere most clearly to this division.

Hence, it is not without probability that philosophy is likened to a fruitful garden, when the physical part is compared with the growth of plants, the ethical part with the ripeness of the fruits, and the logical part with the strength of the walls. Others say that it is similar to an egg, namely, that the ethical part is similar to the yolk, which, according to others, is the germ, the physical part is similar to the protein, which, as you know, is food for the yolk [i.e.], and logical - with an outer shell. Since the parts of philosophy are mutually inseparable, the plants, on the one hand, are considered separately from the fruits and the walls are separated from the plants, then Posidonius considered it more appropriate to liken philosophy to a living being, namely: the physical part - blood and meat, the logical part - bones and muscles, the ethical – soul" (p. 63-64) (8).

As can be seen from the quoted quotations, the ancient authors were close to a correct understanding of the relationship between the parts of philosophy. Indeed, philosophy in its full form can be divided into three parts according to three "subjects": the object of activity, the subject of activity and the activity itself, more precisely, its means-methods.

So, the content of philosophy consists of the most general ideas about the world as a whole, its categorical structure, about a person and the society in which he lives, about the ways in which a person works or masters the world. Graphically, the subject of philosophy looks like this:

Three "parts" of the subject of philosophy can be distinguished:

1. The world as a whole (objective reality), its categorical structure (an objective system of categorical definitions of the world).

2. Man and society (subjective reality) (9).

3. Activity, interaction of the subject with the object, methods and directions of activity (thinking, knowledge, practice, art).

According to the three "parts" of the subject, three "parts" of philosophy can be distinguished:

1. The doctrine of the world as a whole and its categorical structure is an ideological "part".

2. The doctrine of man and society - philosophical anthropology and social philosophy.

3. The doctrine of the forms and methods of activity - the methodological "part".

As a worldview, philosophy gives the most general idea of the world as a whole and its categorical structure. The subject of this "part" of philosophy is the objective reality, the world as it exists by itself, independently of man and humanity. The ideological aspect of philosophy highlights its objectivity, impartiality. In this "part" it aspires to the ideal of "scientific" philosophy.

As a doctrine of man and society, philosophy implements the principle of "know thyself" and orients the development of man and society in a certain direction. This aspect of philosophy could be called ideological. He discovers its active, active, subjective character, its partiality.

As a doctrine of the forms and methods of activity, philosophy serves as a general method of cognition and practice. It is not enough to have an idea about the world as a whole, it is not enough to know what a person wants, it is also necessary to develop issues of successful activity for the development (cognition and transformation) of the world. The subject of the methodological "part" of philosophy is human activity in its diverse forms, in other words, the interaction of the subject (man and society) with the object (objective world). At the center of philosophical methodology is the problem of the relationship between the ideal and the real as a concentrated expression of the general problem of the relationship between the subjective and the objective. Philosophical methodology includes:

1. Teaching about thinking.

2. The doctrine of knowledge.

3. Teaching about practice.

4. Teaching about art.

5. The doctrine of creativity.

In the doctrine of thinking, the question of the idea is central.

In the doctrine of knowledge, the question of truth is central.

In the doctrine of practice, the question of the good, of value, is central.

In the doctrine of art, the central issue is the question of beauty, beauty.

Each of these "parts" of philosophical methodology has its own system of specific categories-concepts.

Philosophy, like any other branch of human activity, develops, becomes more complex, and, consequently, differentiates within itself. There is a process of differentiation of philosophy and specialization of its individual parts. On the other hand, from time to time there are philosophical systems that "work" towards the integration of philosophical ideas. Differentiation and integration of philosophy are two sides of a single process of its formation and development.

A peculiar division of labor between philosophers has long since developed. They were divided into specialist philosophers (specializing in any one area of philosophy) and systematist philosophers, who strive to cover the whole wealth of philosophical ideas with a single mind's eye. Both those and other philosophers are needed by modern society.

Approximately the same situation is observed in natural science. Thus, speaking in defense of Hegel, the US physicist B. Steferding holds the idea that the historical misunderstanding between the natural sciences and Hegelian philosophy needs to be revised. According to him, Hegel, being a great philosopher, "set himself the same tasks that the theoreticians of natural science set themselves, namely, to bring known facts into a coherent system." According to him, "95% of all modern natural science research is aimed at expanding knowledge about the facts, and only a few of the natural scientists are concerned with bringing facts and data into an all-encompassing system" (10).

D. Diderot expressed interesting thoughts about the philosophers-collectors of facts and systematists. He wrote: "On the one hand, to collect, on the other hand, to connect facts - two very difficult activities; philosophers and distributed these activities among themselves. Some devote their lives to collecting materials, they are useful and industrious workers; others, proud builders, rush to use them. But time has up to now overthrown almost all the constructions of rational philosophy. Doomed to work in the dust, the worker sooner or later brings out of the dungeon, where he works blindly, a block that is destructive for this architecture, invented by the head method; it collapses, and only piles of rubble remain, until another bold genius undertakes a new combination...

We have distinguished two kinds of philosophy: experimental philosophy and rational philosophy. One is blindfolded, she always stumbles, she takes everything she gets her hands on, and, in the end, stumbles upon precious things. Another picks up this precious material and tries to kindle a torch from it; but until now this imaginary torch has served her worse than her rival's groping; this is natural.

Experience indefinitely multiplies its searches, it acts continuously; he is invariably looking for phenomena, while the mind follows the path of analogies. Experimental philosophy does not know what it will come across in the work and what will not be; but she works tirelessly. On the contrary, rational philosophy weighs the possibilities, pronounces its judgment and falls silent..."(11).

If we take the development of philosophy over long periods of time, we will see that from time to time all-encompassing systems of philosophy appeared. In ancient Greece, such an all-encompassing system was the philosophy of Aristotle. In modern times, every major philosopher claimed to create a system of philosophical knowledge. Systematic teachings left Descartes, Spinoza, Hobbes, Locke, Kant. Hegel has truly become the Aristotle of modern times.

3.PHILOSOPHICAL PLURALISM, VARIETY OF PHILOSOPHICAL DOCTRINES AND TRENDS

The variety of philosophical teachings and trends - from the variety of human types, characters and the variety of forms of activity. Even Aristotle noticed that the views of the philosopher are determined by what he does. About Pythagoras and the Pythagoreans, he wrote: "... the so-called Pythagoreans, having taken up mathematics, were the first to develop it and, having mastered it, began to consider its beginnings to be the beginnings of everything that exists" (12).

The most famous division of philosophers is the division into materialists and idealists. It is also the oldest. Already Plato divided the philosophers in this way.

According to A.N. Chanyshev, "Plato was the first philosopher in the history of philosophy who realized that the history of philosophy is the history of the struggle between two types of philosophers (who later became known as materialists and idealists). Of the philosophers, "some people draw everything from heaven and from the region of the invisible to earth ... assert that there is only that which allows touch and touch, and recognize bodies and being as one and the same", while others insist that " true being is some intelligible and incorporeal ideas" (Sophist, 246 AB).

At the same time, Plato speaks of the struggle between these two types of philosophers: the first all those who say that there is something incorporeal are "poured with contempt", while the second do not recognize the body as being. "Regarding this (i.e., what to take for being: bodies or ideas. - A. Ch.) between both parties, - Plato concludes his story about two types of philosophers, - there is a strong struggle" (ibid.). Plato is on the side of the second philosophers. He calls them "the meeker ones" (246 AC)." - A.N. Chanyshev. From an unpublished manuscript on the history of ancient philosophy.

Materialism and idealism are different mainly because of the difference in their objects. The object of materialistic philosophy is nature and everything else it considers through the "prism" of nature. The main object of attention of idealistic philosophy are the highest forms of human, spiritual, social life. If the spiritual life of human society is taken as the basis, then this is objective idealism. If the spiritual life of the individual is taken as the basis, then this is subjective idealism.

Materialists proceed from nature, from matter, and explain the phenomena of the human spirit on the basis of material causes. Idealists proceed from the phenomena of the human spirit, from thinking, and on their basis explain everything else. In short, the materialists go from the world to man and his mind, while the idealists go from man to the world.

Idealists try to explain the lower through the higher, while materialists, on the contrary, try to explain the higher through the lower.

Materialists view the ideal as a cast, a reflection of the real. Idealists, on the other hand, regard the real as a cast product of the ideal. Both of them are right in their own way. Materialists absolutize the cognitive ability of a person (after all, in cognition, we translate the real into an ideal plan; the ideal, obtained in the process of cognition, only repeats the real, corresponds to it, separates what is divided in the object and connects what is connected in the object; in cognition we adapt to the world, trying to merge with it, to dissolve in it). Idealists absolutize the man's control-transforming ability (in control-transformative activity we translate the ideal into a real plan; the real, obtained as a result of such activity, only repeats the ideal, corresponds to it;

There is one more difference between materialism and idealism, about which A.I. Herzen: "... idealism sought to destroy material being, to take it for dead, for a ghost, for a lie, for nothing, perhaps because it is very little to be one accident of essence. Idealism saw and recognized one universal, generic, essence, human reason, estranged from everything human; materialism, just as one-sided, went straight to the destruction of everything immaterial, denied the universal, saw the separation of the brain, in empiricism a single source of knowledge, and recognized the truth in some particulars, in some things, tangible and visible; for him there was a rational person, but there was neither reason nor humanity ... "(13).

It should also be pointed out that materialism and idealism are very different in their value orientations. "Impossible by logical arguments," L.N. Gumilyov - to reconcile people whose views on the origin and essence of the world are polar, because they come from fundamentally different worldviews. Some perceive the material world and its diversity as a blessing, others as an unconditional evil..."(14). You don't have to look far for examples. Here is Hegel's opinion: "... everything spiritual is better than any product of nature" (15). The biologist R. Mayer was of the opposite opinion. "Nature in its simple truth," he wrote, "is greater and more beautiful than any creation of human hands, than all the illusions of the created spirit" (!6).

Another well-known division of philosophers is into rationalists, empiricists and irrationalists.

Rationalists tend to order, love it and absolutize it. Accordingly, they absolutize knowledge, they try to interpret everything unknown from the standpoint of known, available knowledge.

Irrationalists, on the contrary, do not like the usual order of things, are prone to disorder, ready to allow anything. Irrationalists are lovers of paradoxes, riddles, mysticism, and so on. They absolutize ignorance, the sphere of the unknown, the unknown, the mystery.

Rationalism and irrationalism is logic and intuition, rationality and alogism elevated to the rank of a philosophical concept or consciously accepted as methodological guidelines, paradigms.

Empiricism -absolutization of the intermediate (between logic and intuition) way of thinking, probabilistic approach. By virtue of its intermediate character, empiricism can gravitate towards rationalism, being, so to speak, rationalistic, and towards irrationalism, being irrationalistic.

The difference between rationalism and irrationalism is not only in their relation to order and disorder. The word "rationalism" comes from the French "rationalisme", which in turn comes from the Latin "rationalis", and the latter from the Latin "ratio". One of the main meanings of the word "ratio" is reason. Accordingly, rationalism is often understood as a concept that affirms the supremacy of reason in human life. And irrationalism by contradiction is considered as a concept that rejects the supremacy of reason in human life. Who is right? The indisputable authority of reason seems obvious and, on the contrary, it is strange why people, philosophers again and again attack reason, reject its claims to supremacy, etc. etc.

There is a contradiction in the fact that the mind controls a person, his behavior. On the one hand, it is clear that the main threads of human behavior control are concentrated in the mind. But, on the other hand, how can a "part" (and the mind is only a "part" of a person, albeit the main one, but still a "part") manage, "twist" the whole?

Yes, indeed, the mind is only a "part", but one that makes the whole whole. Mind is an integral "property" of a person that makes him whole, i.e. in a certain sense, he is both a part and a whole, is a link between the "parts" of a person and a person as a whole.

Rationalists love Cartesian "I think, therefore I am." Irrationalists are closer to Shakespeare's words: "There are many, friend Horace, in the world such that our wise men never dreamed of."

Rationalists focus on the supremacy of reason, and irrationalists - on its limitations, on the fact that the mind is smaller than the person himself, less than life, and therefore cannot be the supreme leader of life. Both are right in their own way. The truth, as always, is somewhere in the middle. A person, on the one hand, tries to be guided in his behavior by the arguments of reason, and, on the other hand, sometimes behaves like an unreasonable being, devoid of reason, or even simply insane, as feeling, enjoying or suffering, as willing or weak-willed, etc. .

Both the neglect of reason and the orientation only to reason are inhuman, if not inhuman.

Philosophers are also divided into dogmatists and skeptics. Philosophers-dogmatists develop their own ideas or state others' ideas and defend them, i.e. argue mainly in the spirit of positive, constructive, affirmative philosophizing. On the contrary, skeptical philosophers are tuned mainly to the wave of critical, destructive philosophizing. They themselves do not develop ideas, but only criticize others. The dogmatist philosophers are the inventor philosophers or expounder philosophers, and the skeptical philosophers are cleaner philosophers, garbage philosophers.

Critical philosophical reflection is very useful for defining and clarifying the boundaries of philosophizing, for clarifying what philosophy can and cannot do. Pikes in philosophy are just as necessary as carp. That's what the pike is for, so that the crucian does not doze off - says the proverb. In antiquity there was a whole school of such philosophers. The titles of the works of the famous skeptic philosopher Sextus Empiricus are interesting: "Against the Logicians", "Against the Physicists", "Against the Scientists".

Extreme dogmatists are no longer philosophers, but people who affirm and defend ideas in spite of any circumstances, without taking into account specific conditions. They do not tolerate any objection and do not tolerate any criticism. Extreme dogmatists are either fanatics or people with ossified rational thinking. Extreme skeptics are also no longer philosophers, but people who do not believe in anything, subjecting everything to crushing, annihilating criticism. These are either spiteful critics who do not like everything, or very suspicious people.

The following division of philosophers also deserves attention: into subjectivists, objectivists and methodologists, depending on the main subject of philosophizing. Philosophers-objectivists focus on worldview problems, on understanding the external world. These include most materialists, natural philosophers, ontologists. Philosophers-subjectivists focus on the problems of man and society. These include most idealists, philosophers of life, existentialists. Finally, methodological philosophers comprehend primarily the forms and means of human activity. These are Kantians, positivists, neo-positivists,pragmatists, representatives of linguistic philosophy, philosophers of science.

In the last hundred or two hundred years, philosophers have appeared who, figuratively speaking, serve the connection of philosophy with other forms of culture. Philosophy does not exist in a vacuum. As a part of culture, it is closely connected with its other parts. Human culture as such is united and diverse. If we imagine it as a discrete-continuous field, then some "areas" are clearly distinguished on it - science, art, practice, religion and, of course, our philosophy.

These "sections" of the cultural field, on the one hand, are relatively independent, independent of each other, on the other hand, they are closely connected with each other and have many intermediate links-transitions between them. Philosophy, for example, smoothly passes into science, and science into philosophy. On the one hand, scientizing philosophers work in philosophy (philosophers of science, methodological philosophers, specializing in the problems of scientific knowledge), on the other hand, philosophizing scientists work in science, developing problems of general scientific and particular scientific methodology. We see the same close connection between philosophy and art.

There are philosophers who specialize exclusively in the philosophical understanding of art and literature, and there are philosophizing art historians and artists. Now, if we take philosophy and practice, we will clearly see, on the one hand, pragmatic philosophers, instrumental philosophers, for example, and, on the other, philosophizing politicians, statesmen, managers, inventors, engineers and other practical specialists. If we talk about transitional links between philosophy and religion, then there are also many of them. There are theologians, religious philosophers, and there are philosophizing theologians and clergymen. on the other hand, philosophizing scientists work in science, developing problems of general scientific and particular scientific methodology. We see the same close connection between philosophy and art.

There are philosophers who specialize exclusively in the philosophical understanding of art and literature, and there are philosophizing art historians and artists. Now, if we take philosophy and practice, we will clearly see, on the one hand,pragmatic,philosophers,instrumenta l philosophers, for example, and, on the other, philosophizing politicians, statesmen, managers, inventors, engineers and other practical specialists. If we talk about transitional links between philosophy and religion, then there are also many of them. There are theologians, religious philosophers, and there are philosophizing theologians and clergymen. on the other hand, philosophizing scientists work in science, developing problems of general scientific and particular scientific methodology. We see the same close connection between philosophy and art.

There are philosophers who specialize exclusively in the philosophical understanding of art and literature, and there are philosophizing art historians and artists. Now, if we take philosophy and practice, we will clearly see, on the one hand, pragmatic philosophers, instrumental philosophers, for example, and, on the other, philosophizing politicians, statesmen, managers, inventors, engineers and other practical specialists. If we talk about transitional links between philosophy and religion, then there are also many of them. There are theologians, religious philosophers and there are philosophizing theologians and clergymen. Developing problems of general scientific and particular scientific methodology.

We see the same close connection between philosophy and art. There are philosophers who specialize exclusively in the philosophical understanding of art and literature, and there are philosophizing art critics and artists. Now, if we take philosophy and practice, we will clearly see, on the one hand, pragmatic philosophers, instrumental philosophers, for example, and, on the other, philosophizing politicians, statesmen, managers, inventors, engineers and other practical specialists. If we talk about transitional links between philosophy and religion, then there are also many of them. There are theologians,religious philosophers, and there are philosophizing theologians and clergymen. developing problems of general scientific and particular scientific methodology. We see the same close connection between philosophy and art. There are philosophers who specialize exclusively in the philosophical understanding of art and literature, and there are philosophizing art critics and artists. Now, if we take philosophy and practice, we will clearly see, on the one hand, pragmatic philosophers, instrumental philosophers, for example, and, on the other, philosophizing politicians, statesmen, managers, inventors, engineers and other practical specialists.

If we talk about transitional links between philosophy and religion, then there are also many of them. There are theologians, religious philosophers, and there are philosophizing theologians and clergymen. We see the same close connection between philosophy and art. There are philosophers who specialize exclusively in the philosophical understanding of art and literature, and there are philosophizing art critics and artists. Now, if we take philosophy and practice, we will clearly see, on the one hand,pragmatic,philosophers,instrumental philosophers, for example, and on the other,philosophizing, politicians,statesmen,managers,inventors, engineers and other practical specialists. If we talk about transitional links between philosophy and religion, then there are also many of them. There are theologians, religious philosophers, and there are philosophizing theologians and clergymen. We see the same close connection between philosophy and art. There are philosophers who specialize exclusively in the philosophical understanding of art and literature, and there are philosophizing art historians and artists. Now, if we take philosophy and practice, we will clearly see, on the one hand, pragmatic philosophers, instrumental philosophers, for example, and, on the other, philosophizing politicians, statesmen, managers, inventors, engineers and other practical specialists.

If we talk about transitional links between philosophy and religion, then there are also many of them. There are theologians, religious philosophers, and there are philosophizing theologians and clergymen. Now, if we take philosophy and practice, we will clearly see, on the one hand, pragmatic philosophers, instrumental philosophers, for example, and, on the other, philosophizing politicians, statesmen, managers, inventors, engineers and other practical specialists. If we talk about transitional links between philosophy and religion, then there are also many of them. There are theologians, religious philosophers, and there are philosophizing theologians and clergymen.

 Now, if we take philosophy and practice, we will clearly see, on the one hand, pragmatic philosophers, instrumental philosophers, for example, and, on the other, philosophizing politicians, statesmen, managers, inventors, engineers and other practical specialists. If we talk about transitional links between philosophy and religion, then there are also many of them. There are theologians, religious philosophers, and there are philosophizing theologians and clergymen.

And, finally, there is a very small number of philosophers who are difficult to attribute to any one type, direction. These are the so-called pure philosophers, systematic philosophers, creators of comprehensive philosophical systems. We talked about them in the previous section. These philosophers are omnivorous in a good way, their views-interests, sympathies-antipathies are quite balanced, and it is they who deserve the title of philosophers to the greatest extent, i.e. people striving for wisdom, sages.

4. PRACTICAL PHILOSOPHY

The significance of practical philosophy stems from the fundamental fact that thought can directly influence action: either induce a person to action, or, on the contrary, slow down, stop action, turn away from it. The purpose of practical philosophy: to encourage people with the help of thought to right, good actions and to turn away from erroneous, bad actions. More precisely, practical philosophy is a philosophy that aims to influence people with the power of thought through the word, persuasion - in the process of live communication(consultation-conversations, interviews, discussions, analysis of a specific situation). A practical philosopher (like a practical psychologist, psychoanalyst, doctor, priest, lawyer) organizes a counseling-interview-confession service. His task: counseling and interviewing on the main issues of life,

It must be kept in mind that practical philosophy is not the same as the practical role of philosophy. Philosophy as a whole has a certain practical impact on people's lives. And mostly indirectly, through science, invention, politics, economics, art, literature. Practical philosophy is that part of philosophy that tries to directly influence people's lives, through philosophical texts and speeches, through live communication between philosophers and people.

Practical philosophy, in the exact sense of the word, was practiced professionally by a few: some sophists in ancient Greece and some philosophers who used philosophical argument in their individual and collective conversations for various practical purposes.

In a broad sense, practical philosophy includes texts and speeches by various authors containing philosophical arguments, thoughts about life, man, about the attitude to the world, addressed to all people and having practical meaning, encouraging action or averting it. These texts and speeches, as a rule, do not have the nature of research, but contain reasoning, individual thoughts and recommendations ... In this second meaning, "practical philosophy" has a rich history and traditions. Many philosophers of the past have left texts that have a practical philosophical meaning. And not only philosophers, but also other writers: fiction writers, scientists, historians, psychologists, politicians, etc.

Unfortunately, practical philosophy (in its basic meaning) is still in its infancy. Society is only now beginning to realize that philosophy can directly (without intermediaries of various kinds) influence the affairs and destinies of people, that philosophers can work with people - like psychologists, psychoanalysts, doctors, priests.

We, philosophers, face a truly historic task: to create an institution of practical philosophers, to create a fashion for philosophers, just as a fashion for psychologists has already been created ...

Speaking in more detail, the need for the institution of a practical philosopher is dictated by the following:

1. A philosopher, unlike representatives of other professions (psychologists, doctors, lawyers, sexologists, priests, etc.), considers a person holistically, in all his life manifestations. It is he who is able to talk to a person as a person, take into account all aspects of human existence-experience and, as it were, conduct all the tools of influence on a person. A psychologist-psychoanalyst is looking for a solution to human problems in the psyche, a doctor - in restoring health, a lawyer - in the effective use of legislation, etc. Only a philosopher can judge which means should be used in certain situations. And it is he who can offer the complex use of various means, that is, to coordinate and conduct.

(Many people speak and write about a person: writers, scientists of various specialties, religious figures, philosophers Writers-artists depict a person exclusively from the subjective side. Scientists examine him as an object. They are objectivists. Religious figures speak and write about a person only in connection with their belief in the supernatural, for them a person is an actor-subject insofar as he embodies, realizes the otherworldly, superhuman principle. These are all one-sided points of view.

Only a philosopher can handle a comprehensive view of a person. For him, a person is both a subject and an object, both one and not one, both "I", and "we", and the individual, and the human race. Such a view of a person is due to the specifics of the philosopher as a universal thinker.

Of course, philosophers can specialize and be limited in their preferences. Nevertheless, in comparison with other "human scientists", they are more focused on universalism in their view of man. At least, it is among them that there are thinkers who aspire to this universalism. Paraphrasing the well-known statement of Pico della Mirandola "who is not a philosopher, he is not a man", let's say: it is the philosopher and only the philosopher who can fully answer the question "what is a man?".)

2. In addition, the philosopher has such a means of solving human problems that no representative of any other human-oriented activity professionally has. That

medium is thought. A professional philosopher is a person who has made thinking (reasoning, argumentation, persuasion, criticism) his profession. And it is he, only he, who can professionally use thought-thinking as a means of influencing a person to solve his problems.

3. It must be borne in mind that philosophy is invisibly present in the minds of people, whether they want it or not. People discuss philosophical problems in one way or another without calling them philosophical. These discussions are mostly unqualified and ignorant. A whole sea of pseudo-philosophical reasoning can be found in television and radio programs, in films, in books, newspapers and magazines. In addition, many human scientists (psychologists, doctors, lawyers, priests, etc.), in addition to purely professional conversations and recommendations, conduct purely philosophical conversations with their clients and give philosophical advice. They work, essentially, in the field of practical philosophy.

Naturally, all these discussions and recommendations in most cases leave much to be desired. And where are we professional philosophers? - We either have a cabal (we rotate in a narrow circle of our colleagues), or we teach philosophy. The whole vast world of living, worldly, practical, natural philosophy remains outside our attention, understanding, and our interests. So let's reverse this situation, let's go to the people, we will work directly with people, together with them solve their fundamental questions of life. Not with the masses, not with the audience (as in the case of students or readers), but with each individual who wishes! The essence of practical philosophy is precisely this: in exclusivity, in targeting, in an individual approach.

A. V. Sokolov wrote back in 1988: "In order to demonstrate practical usefulness, philosophy must provide a product that meets the needs of individual everyday practice. "Practical philosophy" can serve as such a product. Philosophy can be useful to a person as life teaching, as wisdom. In this function, it is able to successfully compete with religion, which also acts in relation to the individual as a life teaching. Philosophy is able to give life wisdom, rationally justified, arising from a theoretical worldview, while religious life teaching is based on an irrationally perceived anthropomorphic, mythological worldview.

A significant shortcoming of the current stage in the development of philosophy in the USSR is precisely the absence in it of such a "practical philosophy" that would correspond to the demands of everyday human practice." (See: The nature and ways of connecting philosophy with life. [abstracts for a scientific conference]. M., 1988, pp. 61-62.)

4. Some philosophers believe that philosophy should not condescend to the individual. Here is what, for example, O.G. Drobnitsky: "Philosophy ... due to the extreme generality of the issues it solves, cannot claim to be a daily mentor of a person in private everyday situations. Consideration of the problems of being on the scale of mankind, history, which is part of the task of philosophy, should not be deduced to specific circumstances, deriving solutions for all occasions. In everyday situations, a person does not

reason like a philosopher, and not only because it is impossible to raise the worldly consciousness of everyone to the level of ultimate abstractions, but because the life position of an individual in the vicissitudes of personal experience cannot always be directly derived from his worldview. Attempts in all cases to establish such a strict dependence can only lead to pedantic doctrinairism, vulgarizing the very concept of philosophy." (See: Sat. "Science and morality", M., 1971. S. 290-291).

Such a view of philosophy is conditioned, on the one hand, by its understanding as being very far from a particular person, and, on the other hand, by understanding the problems of a particular person as insignificant for philosophy. In both cases, we are dealing with a kind of philosophical Platonism, i.e. with the absolutization of the general-universal and the underestimation of the individual, separate, specific. Yes, indeed, philosophy deals with questions of ultimate generality. But after all, every single person thinks about such questions. There is no common without separate, singular, just as there is no single without common.

Any most fundamental question is peripetic, situational, depends on the specific life of a particular person, on his characteristics and the characteristics of his life. And, on the contrary, any specific vital problem is connected by thousands of threads with the solution of general issues.

The task of a practical philosopher: to constantly highlight, to show this connection between the general and the separate, the connection between fundamental philosophical and concrete life issues. A parallel can be drawn here between the practical philosopher and the judge. The judge is engaged in the fact that he compares the specific data in the case with the rules of law and, on the basis of this, makes a decision. And a philosopher, consulting, leading a conversation, must not only bring the particular under the general, but establish (find-consider-evaluate) the connection between the particular and the general. (Here Kant's "ability to judge" comes to mind. Here is what A. Gulyga wrote about it: "If reason sets the rules, then the ability to judge gives the ability to use these rules in each individual case; in fact, this is the mind, ingenuity. know the laws; if he formally applies them, then it can turn out "right, but bad", must be judged wisely, considering all the circumstances of the case. In folklore, the image of a simpleton is recorded, which acts as a standard, and therefore constantly gets into a mess. Kant would say that the simpleton lacks the determining faculty of judgment, as he called the ability to apply the general to the particular." –

5. The contact of a professional philosopher with a non-philosopher is still limited either by teaching philosophy, or through philosophical texts, or by oral presentations in front of a particular audience, or by a few communications at different forums (conferences, seminars, symposiums, etc.). In some cases, the contact is one-sided, in others it is blurred in various collective communications. Truly communication between a philosopher and a non-philosopher is possible only in an individual lively conversation, specially designed for this. Of course, Plato was right when he pointed out the insufficiency of philosophical texts and the need for a living contact between a philosopher and a non-philosopher. In the Phaedra he wrote:

"This, Phaedrus, is a bad feature of writing, truly similar to painting: its creations stand as if alive, and ask them - they are majestically and proudly silent. It is the same with compositions: you think that they speak like rational beings, but if someone asks about something from what they say, wanting to learn it, they always answer the same thing. Any work, once written down, is in circulation everywhere - both among people who understand, and, equally, among those who are not at all befitting to read, and it does not know with whom it should speak and with whom it should not. If he is neglected or unjustly scolded, he needs the help of his father, but he is not able to defend himself, nor help himself ...

Well, why not take a look at how another composition arises, the brother of the first, and how much better and more powerful it is by its nature?

(...) This is the composition that, as knowledge is acquired, is written in the soul of the student; it is able to defend itself and at the same time it knows how to talk to whom it should, it knows how to keep silent.

Are you talking about the living and animated speech of a knowledgeable person, the reflection of which can rightly be called written speech?

- Quite right (...) even better (writing texts - L.B.), in my opinion, such activities will become if you use the art of dialectics: having taken a suitable soul, such a person with knowledge of the matter plants and sows in it speeches that can help both ourselves and the sower, for they are not barren, they have a seed that will give birth to new speeches in the souls of other people, capable of making this seed immortal forever, and its owner as happy as a person can be (my italics - L.B. .)." (274B-277A)

Here is how T.V. Vasilyeva comments on these words of Plato: to help resolve the perplexity that has arisen - but the text can only repeat again and again what has already been said. A live conversation is more perfect - the interlocutor is in front of you, you see him and can adapt to him, all perplexities can be resolved in the course of the conversation - what is learned in the process of such independent work in a live interview, then cuts into the memory firmly, and most importantly, begins to generate in the soul of the listener the ability to have an internal conversation with oneself - this is the meaning of Socrates' speech "(TV Vasilyeva. Athenskaya School of Philosophy. M., 1985. P. 109).

To what T.V. Vasilyeva said, let us add that a lively conversation is important not only for the interlocutor of the philosopher, but also for the philosopher himself (as Plato rightly points out). In it, the philosopher draws new information, new thoughts and ideas, is charged with creative energy, as is the case with an artist performing in front of a live audience.

6. By introducing the institution of practical philosophers, a good ancient tradition is being revived. In ancient times there was already a similar institution of practical philosophers. They are sophists, teachers of wisdom, teachers of life. True, there were those among them who taught false wisdom, idle talk, and sophistry. Nevertheless, initially there was a rational grain in the activities of the sophists. With their conversations and wise advice, they really helped people.

The goals of the work (consulting-conversation) of a practical philosopher:

1. Clarification of the meaning of life.

2. Assistance in finding vital answers (where to go? what to do? which way to choose? what is good?).

3. Creation of intellectual preconditions for a way out of conflict situations (everyday, professional, creative, love, family...).

4. Philosophical therapy (consolation and treatment with philosophy).

5. Prevention (prevention) of possible erroneous decisions, immoral acts, crimes, suicide.

Methods and forms of work of a practical philosopher:

1. Philosophical consultation (questions and answers).

2. Conversation, discussion, dialogue.

3. Analysis of specific situations.

4. A heart-to-heart talk (to give an opportunity to express everything that has accumulated, sore, to check one's thoughts with the thoughts of philosophers, to eliminate or minimize gaps, white spots in understanding oneself and others).

5. Frank conversation (with the obligatory condition of secrecy)

6. Practical advice, explanations, argumentation, persuasion, criticism.

Basic Methods for Discussing Problems: the method of antitheses and the method of alternatives/variants.

When using the antithesis method, a thesis is put forward (by a philosopher or interlocutor); arguments for and against the thesis are stated; the final conclusion is left to the interlocutor.

When using the method of alternatives / options, different alternatives for answering a question or options for solving a problem are put forward; then these alternatives/options are discussed; the final choice of alternative/option is given to the interlocutor.

The following methods can also be used:

1) the method of story-lecture (the philosopher is active - the interlocutor is passive);

2) the method of listening-confession (the philosopher is passive - the interlocutor is active);

3) the mixed method of lecture-listening (alternate activity of the philosopher and the interlocutor).

These methods can be called storytelling methods. Their goal is to give a person a chance to speak out, to confess, or to satisfy his curiosity, to eliminate the informational hunger he is experiencing.

Narrative methods are not as effective as antithesis/alternative/option methods. Nevertheless, they can be used if the interlocutor prefers the narrative style of conversation to reasoning-argumentation-analysis.

In addition to these methods, the method of questions and answers is very effective.

Questions can be asked by both the philosopher and the interlocutor.

A practical philosopher must be comprehensively educated, know and be able to do a lot, be a know-it-all and know-it-all in a good sense. Specifically, in a consulting-interview situation, he should be a bit of a psychologist, a bit of a doctor, a bit of an artist, a bit of a coach, etc. He needs this, first of all, so that he can perform the functions of a coordinator-conductor in cases where the client only in his services, but also in the services of other specialists.

Rules of behavior of a philosopher in a situation of consulting-interview:

1. Maximum respect for the client.

2. Confidentiality of the conversation, the unconditional secrecy of confession.

3. Compliance with the principle of "do no harm."

Organization of the work of practical philosophers. Centers of practical philosophy.

Practical philosophers can work both individually and unite with others, organizing for this purpose centers of practical philosophy.

Working conditionspractical philosopher can be very different: from receiving a client in the office to communicating in an informal setting (on a walk, when visiting a museum, exhibition, theater, concert), at home, while traveling, at a meal, etc.)

In the future, an association of practical philosophers should be created and rules for admission to the association should be worked out. Such an association could perform functions similar to those of a bar association. This is necessary, first of all, in order to create a barrier to the penetration of charlatans and dilettantes into practical philosophy. Of course, only qualified philosophers (having a diploma of a higher educational institution in the specialty "philosophy" or a diploma of a candidate [doctor] of philosophical sciences) should be allowed to work as practical philosophers. Ideally, practical philosophers should have special training, i.e., in addition to general philosophical education, they should receive special education precisely as practical philosophers.

Centers for Practical Philosophyare created with the aim of organizing a philosophical consulting-interview service, i.e. providing services to the population on issues of practical philosophy (life-death, choosing a profession, creativity, love, marriage and family, relationships between parents and children, philosophical therapy [using philosophy for the purpose of healing , consolation], prevention of drug addiction, suicide (suicide), crimes, immoral acts, etc.).

Areas of work of the Centers:

1) provision of services to the population (philosophical counseling [questions and answers], interview [exchange of opinions, dialogue], analysis of specific situations, confession [frank conversation], commentary-evaluation [in a situation of visiting, examining something]);

2) individual teaching of philosophy (including practical wisdom) according to special programs;

3) research work in the field of practical philosophy.

Practical philosophy in the history of human thought

The works of practical philosophy include those that contain thoughts about life, man, about the attitude to the world, addressed to all people and having practical meaning, that is, encouraging or repelling action. These works, as a rule, do not have the nature of research, but contain reasoning, individual thoughts and recommendations-advice.

Confucius, many ancient philosophers, M. Montaigne, F. Bacon, A. Schopenhauer wrote in the spirit of practical philosophy... In a certain sense, the books of the American Dale Carnegie and our Vladimir Levy can be attributed to the works of practical philosophy.

The sleep of reason breeds monsters. A disdainful attitude towards philosophy and philosophers is a state close to the sleep of the mind. Russia is still experiencing monstrous upheavals. Is it not because, apart from everything else, it is in philosophical hibernation, does not have a developed philosophical culture?! It may be said: we have a history of Russian philosophy, there are dozens of outstanding names, thousands of professional philosophers are working. Yes, all this is good, but not enough! Philosophy in both tsarist and communist Russia developed under the vigilant eye of the state. Hence its religious orientation in the pre-October era and the Marxist-scientist - in the post-October. Not a single philosophical school has been created. Great Russia... but without great philosophers, without great philosophical traditions-standards. Isn't it sad? The sleep of reason breeds monsters. It is said about us.

It is not enough for us, philosophers, to publish books, magazines, teaching at universities, universities, secondary educational institutions in order to fully develop, create, actively and powerfully influence society and culture. A permanent independent philosophical institution is what we, Russia, and all mankind need. Philosophy, as a special branch of human culture, must finally find its own institutions, be institutionalized.

The Academy of Philosophy, independent of the state, science, religion, could serve the cause of the institutionalization of philosophy.

The Academy of Philosophy should become the first independent philosophical institution in Russia. Its creation will not automatically lead to the rise of philosophical reason in our country, but will serve as a powerful impetus to its development.

Now specifically about how I see the Academy of Philosophy. I will first outline the aims and tasks of the Academy point by point.

1. The Academy is created with the aim of institutionalizing philosophy, ensuring its independent existence, development as a branch of human culture, elevation in the eyes of society.

The motto of the Academy is that philosophy should exist as an independent branch of culture, regardless of the state, science, religion.

[The independence of the Academy of Philosophy from the state does not mean that it will operate as an isolated institution. Business contacts with state institutions, financial and other assistance from the state are quite possible. The independence of the Academy will be ensured by the absence of its one-sided dependence, by the presence of various sponsors-donors independent of each other.]

The Academy should lay the foundation for the first philosophical school in Russia, i.e. one of the goals of the Academy is to revive the ancient tradition of philosophical schools, as it was in ancient times. The Academy founded by Plato existed for over 900 years, from 385 BC. before 529 AD The Peripatetic school founded by Aristotle also existed intermittently for several hundred years. As a result, we have a wonderful European culture. Here we can draw an analogy between the ancient Olympic Games and their revival in our era on a new basis. Now the Olympic movement is one of the greatest phenomena of human culture. Like the Olympic movement, the tradition of philosophical schools must be revived and developed!

2.   Philosophical pluralism and freethinking are proclaimed and implemented. Philosophers recognize no authority other than the authority of thought. The Academy maintains the spirit of healthy competition of philosophical ideas.

3. In the dispute between science and religion, mysticism, parascience, the Academy takes the side of science. It is the knowledge acquired by scientists that serves as a breeding ground for philosophizing.

4. The Academy does not accept extreme views, rejects gullibility, inertness, abnormality, psychopathology. Her motto is: measure in everything, even in keeping the measure!

5. The Academy pays special attention to the development of the foundations, the

beginnings of philosophy. At the same time, she strives for the inclusiveness of philosophizing.

6. The Academy provides special philosophical education - for youth (secondary), youth (higher) and postgraduate studies.

The Academy should lay the foundation for an organized, institutionalized philosophical education of children. Philosophy can be taught from an early age, as music is taught in music schools or military science in military schools. Children may well perceive and assimilate philosophy. On the other hand, the sooner a person gets acquainted with philosophy and the sooner he masters it, the more capable he will be as a philosopher, the faster and more powerfully his philosophical talent, and perhaps even genius, will develop.

Thanks to its independent status, the Academy will also open unprecedented prospects for the philosophical education of youth and adults. After all, what is philosophical education in our country today? This is the training of students at the philosophical faculties of universities and the training of graduate students in the philosophical graduate school of these faculties and in the system of the Russian Academy of Sciences (at the Institute of Philosophy of the Russian Academy of Sciences, at the Department of Philosophy of the Russian Academy of Sciences, etc.). Here we see the double dependence of philosophy - on the state and science. After all, universities and colleges where there is training in philosophical specialties are mainly state universities and universities.

7 Further, the philosophical specialty in these universities and colleges is present among many other specialties, and they most often represent certain sections of science, scientific knowledge. Philosophical preparation, thus, it is under the strict control of state bodies and non-philosophical, scientific institutions. Take Moscow State University. In its composition, as we know, there is a philosophical faculty. In addition to this faculty, the university has a dozen other faculties - natural sciences and humanitarian sciences. The Faculty of Philosophy is one of twenty! Of course, the educational policy at the university is

determined not by him, but by the scientific faculties surrounding him. The Faculty of Philosophy has, however, relative independence.

But still, this is not the kind of independence that a separate independent philosophical institution could have. there is a philosophy department. In addition to this faculty, the university has a dozen other faculties natural sciences and humanitarian sciences. The Faculty of Philosophy is one of twenty! Of course, it is not he who determines the educational policy at the university, but the scientific faculties surrounding him.

The Faculty of Philosophy has,however,relative independence. But still, this is not the kind of independence that a separate independent philosophical institution could have. there is a philosophy department. In addition to this faculty, the university has a dozen other faculties - natural sciences and humanitarian sciences. The Faculty of Philosophy is one of twenty! Of course, the educational policy at the university is determined not by him, but by the scientific faculties surrounding him. The

Faculty of Philosophy has, however, relative independence. But still, this is not the kind of independence that a separate independent philosophical institution could have Broad philosophical education - for all those interested in philosophy.

8. The independent status of the Academy will also ensure the independent (from the state and science) professional status of philosophers.

The current state of affairs is as follows: the professional status of philosophers is ensured by university diplomas, the award of scientific degrees of candidate and doctor of philosophy, the academic titles of associate professor and professor, and, finally, membership in the Russian Academy of Sciences and similar institutions. In all these cases, the assessment of the professionalism of a philosopher depends on government officials and officials from science. This is most clearly seen in the example of the Higher Attestation Commission (Higher Attestation Commission) and the Russian Academy of Sciences. The Higher Attestation Commission - being a purely state institution - dictates to philosophers who should be a high professional and who should not be. The Russian Academy of Sciences - in its composition is absolutely non-philosophical - at general meetings, where philosophers make up an insignificant percentage, it determines who should be an academician from philosophy and who should not be.

They refer to the need for generally accepted standards of philosophical education and professionalism. Yes, I agree, such standards are needed in our time. But why these standards must be determined by the state? Is it possible that generally accepted standards can only be adopted by the state (through the Higher Attestation Commission, the Ministry of Education, the Russian Academy of Sciences, etc.)?! After all, there are examples when these standards are set by institutions independent of the state. Diplomas from Cambridge and Oxford in England, Harvard University in the USA are valued all over the world as high standards of education, culture and scholarship. Generally accepted standards of philosophical professionalism can be generally recognized diplomas of an independent philosophical institution.

Moreover, they may not exist in the singular, if there are several authoritative independent philosophical institutions.

Having won sufficient authority in philosophical circles, the Academy of Philosophy may eventually become a "trendsetter". Its diplomas of secondary and higher education, scientific degrees and titles can become universally recognized standards of philosophical education, culture, scholarship.

9. If the Academy of Philosophy is created, it will serve as a good example for the creation of similar philosophical institutions in other countries, will serve the cause of the institutionalization of philosophy throughout the world. And in Russia there should be more than one Academy of Philosophy. Healthy competition between philosophical schools is only for the benefit of philosophy.

10. The Academy should become the mental center of Russia or one of the mental (intellectual) centers of Russia, the world.

The task of the Academy as a mental center is to elevate philosophy in the eyes of society, to make the voice of philosophers as significant as the voice of politicians, scientists, cultural figures, media representatives, and religious figures. People must eventually realize that philosophy is the mind of society. They should treat her with the same respect as they treat their mind.

To the draft charter of the Academy of Philosophy

1. The purpose of the Academy is to ensure the independent existence and development of philosophy as a branch of human culture.

2. The Academy has two departments:

— department of philosophical creativity

— department of philosophical education.

These departments should function in close contact. Pupils, students and graduate students, as a rule, participate in philosophical creativity and research, while professional philosophers participate in the educational process.

3. The Department of Philosophical Research has two directions:

- foundations, beginnings of philosophy

– applied philosophy

4. The department of philosophical education has several levels:

- a stage of broad philosophical education - for all those interested in philosophy and philosophical problems

— stage of secondary education (students)

— stage of higher education (students)

— level of professional training (post-graduate students)

5. Structure of the Academy.

The academy is headed by a president elected for life. He appoints the Academy Council, which assists him in matters of administration.

The second and subsequent presidents of the Academy are elected secretly by the Council of the Academy after the death or, in exceptional cases, after the voluntary resignation of the previous president within three months.

The Council of the Academy consists of no less than four and no more than twelve members.

The Council of the Academy can perform the functions of a collegial governing body of the Academy with the written consent of the President of the Academy.

Members of the Council of the Academy perform, as directed by the president, the functions of vice presidents.

DREAMS-FANTASIES

How do I see the Academy of Philosophy?

In Moscow or the Moscow suburbs - an academic campus - two-three-story houses (research and educational buildings, a boarding house for students, students, graduate students and residential buildings for employees) on a site with a small park-garden, a winter garden, with walking alleys, gazebos , sports grounds, swimming pool, treadmills.

Educational and research classes are held in the house / houses and in the park, on the alleys, in the gazebos.

The Academy has a good library and a reading room, a sports hall, workshops, and is equipped with computers and printing equipment. The Academy has a conference hall, where, in addition to regular events, academic evenings, music concerts, etc. are held.

At the Academy there is a philosophical school-college for children from 7 to 17 years old.

The Academy publishes works, journals, writings of pupils and employees, writings of various philosophers.

A philosophical museum is organized at the Academy, a specialized philosophical theater operates.

The museum collects exhibits about the life and work of famous philosophers, works of art that have philosophical value.

Philosophical plays and plays from the life of philosophers are staged in the theater.

The Council of the Academy organizes the competition and awarding of academic degrees and titles in various branches of philosophy.

Membership in the Academy should be the highest recognition of the merits of a philosopher. Membership status is two-stage: corresponding member and full member.

To encourage the most talented philosophers, the Academy establishes various awards.

The Academy organizes competitions for the best essays on selected topics, symposiums, conferences.

Every employee or student at the Academy must systematically engage in general developmental sports.

At the Academy, not only work or study, but also live. For pupils, students and graduate students — a boarding house. For employees - a residential building with apartments or separate residential buildings.

To implement the Academy's project in full, a lot of money is needed, perhaps more than one million dollars. Therefore, it is quite possible that the creation of the Academy can stretch over several large stages (for decades).

At first, an explanatory, propaganda campaign is needed to attract public attention to the project and, accordingly, financial resources for its implementation.

An Academy fund should also be established to accumulate financial resources.

At the first stage, for the establishment of the Academy and its functioning, it is enough to have-rent a small two-three-storey building.

In the future, the architectural ensemble of the academic campus should be built according to a special project. The architectural structures of the academic campus should not be gray, dull, either inside or outside. Their purpose is not only functional. They should delight the eye with their unique beauty. In the rooms there are paintings by artists, portraits, busts of great philosophers.

I invite everyone who is interested in the idea of creating the Academy of Philosophy to express their suggestions, wishes to me personally or on the pages of the CATEGORY magazine.

I invite professional philosophers to cooperate in order to unite efforts to create the Academy of Philosophy. It is necessary to develop a manifesto and charter of the Academy, to prepare competing educational and research programs. Finally, we need candidates for the staff of the Academy.

I think we could start raising funds for the Academy Foundation. If anyone has suggestions on this subject, please contact me (see address and phone number on page 2 of this brochure).

Sponsors, get in touch! By assisting in the creation of the first Academy of Philosophy in Russia, you will become the new Tretyakovs and Mamontovs, inscribe your name in golden letters in the cultural history of Russia.

Send feedback and suggestions to:

Russia, 115583, Moscow, Voronezhskaya st., 9, 110. To Balashov Lev Evdokimovich.Phone: 397-77-91

Notes

1) Philosophy is the highest manifestation of the ability of the living-human to delay the reaction, action, response in order to think about how best to act-act. The most elementary behavior is unconditioned reflex, when there is a minimum distance between sensation and action (for example, pulling the hand away from a hot object immediately after touching). Human behavior is the more difficult, the greater the distance (delay) between perception and action, cognition and practice. Philosophers are those representatives of the human race who personify-materialize this delay to the

greatest extent. To philosophy "we are prompted by a strange need to delay, linger, stop, reflect, do what a busy person sees as idle, idle, scholastic, abstract reasoning from life." (See: A.V. Akhutin. Matter of Philosophy. - In: ARCHE: Yearbook of the cultural-logical seminar / Ed. V.S. Bibler. Issue. 2. M.: Ross. state humane un-t. 1996. S. 72.)

2) Aristotle also pointed out this feature of cognitive activity: "... the truth is said by the one who considers the disconnected to be disconnected and the connected - connected, and the false - the one who thinks the opposite of how things are" (Metaphysics 1051b 3-6). — Aristotle. Op. in 4 t.t. T. 1, M., 1976. S. 250.

3) T. Hill's objection to the logical positivists is fair in this respect. He wrote: "Even if the concepts of "logic" and "science" are considered more broadly than the logical positivists themselves do, still considering philosophy only the logic of science means too narrowing philosophy. Philosophy has always tried to interpret not only one aspect of human experience, but all of its aspects, and human experience contains so much more

than science." (See: T.I. Hill. Modern theories of knowledge. M., 1965. P. 427)

4) In the case of ideas, we can only talk about their possible truth or possible utility. Until an idea is tested empirically or in practice, it has only possible value. A philosophical idea not only cannot be the ultimate truth, but simply the truth. At best, it can lead to truth, to knowledge. For more information about the status of ideas and the criteria for their nomination-consistency, see: Balashov L.E. How do we think? M., 1996. S. 12-26.

5) Note. Ed.: Ethics, physics and logic (dialectics) are meant. This division of philosophy is attributed to Xenocrates. Xenocrates - the successor of Speusippus, who led the Academy in 339-314. BC. Speusippus led the Academy in 347-339. BC. Speusippus is Plato's nephew.

6) Seneca. Moral letters to Lucilius. M., 1977. S. 198.

7) Diogenes Laertes. About the life, teachings and sayings of famous philosophers. M., 1979. S. 68.

8) Sextus Empiricus. Op. in 2 tons T. 1, M., 1975.

9) Man-society is a dual subject in which man plays a decisive role. Man is the primary subject, society is secondary. Man "shines" with his own light, society with its reflected light. On the other hand, these two subjects, like two Magdeburg hemispheres, are inseparable. Man for himself is a subject in all respects. Society is not a subject for itself, much less a subject in all respects. For man, society is primarily an objective reality. Society in relation to nature is a subject; it acts, transforms nature, but in relation to man it is both objective and the essence of something dependent, which is part of man. For example, science, a part of society, cannot exist without individual scientists. The latter make science science! Or: philosophy as collective thinking, on the one hand, seems to exist independently of the individual philosopher, but, on the other hand, does not exist outside the thinking of individual philosophers. It can exist independently of an individual philosopher, but it cannot exist independently of a multitude of individual philosophers.

The greatest reality is not in an individual person and not in society, but in something in between the one and the other: in man-society or in society-man. A man-society is a man living in a society; society-man is a society that realizes itself in an individual person, lives thanks to a person.

10) See: afterword by A.P. Ogurtsov to the 2nd volume of Hegel's Encyclopedia of Philosophical Sciences. — Hegel. Ents. philosophy Sciences. T. 2, M., 1974. S. 619.

11) Diderot D. Selected philosophical works. M., 1941. S. 100-102.

12) Aristotle. Op. T. 1, M., 1976. S. 75 ("Metaphysics", 985b 23-25).

13) Herzen A.I. Collected Op. in 30 tons T. 3. S. 264.

14) Gumilyov L.N. From Russia to Russia. M., 1992. S. 211.

15) Hegel. Op. T. XII. S. 31.

16) Quot. Quoted from: Kuznetsov B.G. A. Einstein. M., 1963. S. 117.

17) For the first time the project of the Academy of Philosophy was published in the 2nd issue (1997) of the magazine "CATEGORIES". Then he published in the journal Common Sense (1998, No. 9). This version of the project is published with changes and additions.

About the cycle "Philosophical Conversations"

The cycle is conceived by the author as a kind of library of philosophical literature on a wide range of problems. It is designed for the reader who is interested in philosophizing in itself. Such a reader can be a philosopher, and a figure in science, culture, and a student, student, graduate student.

The books of the cycle belong to the category of developing literature and can serve as teaching aids for replenishing knowledge of philosophy.

In the cycle "Philosophical Conversations" the author published:

Life, death, immortality. M., 1996. - 96 p.

How do we think? M., 1996. - 60 p.

The world through the eyes of a philosopher. (Categorical picture of the world). M., 1997. - 293 p.

Criticism of Marxism and Communism. M., 1997. - 69 p.

Correspondences and anti-correspondences between categories. M., 1998. - 51 p.

Golden rule of conduct. M., 1996, 1999. - 23 p.

Liberalism and freedom. M., 1999. - 19 p.

About love. M., 2000. - 47 p.

About the books of the series "Philosophical Conversations"

In the book "The World through the Eyes of a Philosopher. (Categorical picture of the world)" offers an original version of the categorical picture of the world, categorical (actually philosophical) logic. This version, on the one hand, continues the line of Aristotle-Hegel in the development of philosophical categories (the study of the categories of thinking, the categorical structure of thinking). On the other hand, it contains a number of new points.

The book is a systematic presentation of the problems of categorical logic, which lie at the foundation of philosophy, philosophical thinking, worldview.

The book is intended for philosophers and scientists dealing with methodological problems. Reading and studying a book is a good intellectual exercise for anyone who wants to improve their intellectual abilities. It can also serve as a textbook on the fundamentals of philosophy for undergraduate and graduate students.

The book "Life, Death, Immortality" is not for lovers of esotericism, mysticism, parascience, etc. It is for those who love philosophy and philosophizing without extraneous additions. The book outlines the realistic concept of life, death, immortality. The author criticizes one-sided views on life only as mortal or immortal. He puts forward and substantiates the idea of "doing" immortality, shows the complex nature of this "doing". Analyzing the phenomenon of real immortality, the author comes to the conclusion that along with potential immortality, there is actual immortality.

In a concentrated form, the main idea of the book looks like this: absolute individual immortality is impossible, but infinite approximation to the ideal of absolute immortality is possible and realizable.

In the book How Do We Think? three topics are covered:

▢ Thinking abilities - mind, reason, Reason.

▢ An idea is a thought of the Mind.

▢ Categories of thinking

The brochure "Golden Rule of Behavior" highlights the main issues of ethics, morality, human society - through the prism of the study of the golden rule of behavior.

"Critique of Marxism and Communism" is a collection of articles and materials from different years. The book is written in the genre of critical philosophizing.

The pamphlet "Correspondences and Anti-Correspondences Between Categories" presents the results of a philosophical discovery. The essence of the discovery is as follows. The author revealed objective correspondences between pairs, families, categories. Correspondences are such, as if the same pra-categories "set out to" be repeated in a different guise in each categorical family.

The brochure "Liberalism and Freedom" deals with the concepts of "liberalism" and "freedom" from the broadest philosophical positions. The author believes that the concept of liberalism must be cleared of layers generated by limited opinions about freedom and opinions that are not related to liberalism itself as the ideology of a free person.

www.ingramcontent.com/pod-product-compliance
Lightning Source LLC
Chambersburg PA
CBHW051446150726
48000CB00005B/2269